WALKS
IN
WENSLEYDALE

HILLSIDE GUIDES

CIRCULAR WALKS IN THE YORKSHIRE DALES

④ WHARFEDALE

⑤ NIDDERDALE

⑥ CRAVEN DALES

⑧ WENSLEYDALE

⑩ WESTERN DALES

⑪ SWALEDALE

OTHER TITLES

① THE WESTMORLAND WAY - Appleby to Arnside

② THE FURNESS WAY - Arnside to Ravenglass

③ THE CUMBERLAND WAY - Ravenglass to Appleby

⑦ CLEVELAND WAY COMPANION - Helmsley to Filey

⑨ THE NORTH BOWLAND TRAVERSE - Slaidburn to Stainforth by David Johnson

⑫ WALKS IN BRONTE COUNTRY - South Pennines

⑬ WALKS ON THE NORTH YORK MOORS - WESTERN

⑭ WALKS ON THE NORTH YORK MOORS - SOUTHERN

⑮ WALKS ON THE NORTH YORK MOORS - NORTHERN

⑯ DALES WAY COMPANION - Ilkley to Bowness

⑰ WALKS IN CALDERDALE · South Pennines

WALKS
IN
WENSLEYDALE

by

Paul Hannon

HILLSIDE PUBLICATIONS

HILLSIDE PUBLICATIONS
11 Nessfield Grove
Exley Head
Keighley
West Yorkshire
BD22 6NU

First published 1987
3rd impression 1989

To MY PARENTS
and my first Wensleydale
memory, of our enjoying
fish and chips in Hawes

Front cover illustration: Upper Falls, Aysgarth
Page 1: on Penhill End

ISBN   0 9509212 7 0

Printed in Great Britain by
Carnmor Print and Design
95/97 London Road
Preston
Lancashire
PR1 4BA

INTRODUCTION

Wensleydale is a broad green valley with innumerable hidden features that more than make amends for its lack of instant grandeur. Here one must make an effort to seek out the attractions, and the ensuing pages lead the discerning walker to a host of splendid sights. An oft-made claim that this is Yorkshire's major dale is a point that Wharfedale would surely debate, unless the many side-valleys and the fertile pastures downstream of the National Park boundary are included. These lesser valleys are something unique to Wensleydale, for Coverdale, Walden, Bishopdale, Raydale and several more are all sizeable dales in their own right. Each contributes its share to the Wensleydale scene. The other of the afore-mentioned aspects is also interesting: the Park boundary stops short of many fine places, not least of all Middleham, Leyburn, Jervaulx and much more still further down-river. Indeed there is enough good country to fill another book of such walks.

The individuality of the valley is also exhibited by its very name - this is the only major dale not to take its title from its river. The Ure - anciently the Yore, a name still applied in some quarters - lost out to the village of Wensley which lies just outside the Park on the road to Middleham. This the Dales' most fertile valley was once a great hunting forest, and other associations with history involve a Brigantes' hill-fort, Iron-age lake-dwellings, a Roman road, a Roman fort, a 13th century abbey, a 14th century castle, a 15th century fortified manor-house, a 16th century beacon-site, a 17th century hall, and traces of lead and coal-mining and of quarrying. Not bad for starters!

The natural attractions surely deserve a mention now. It will be noticed that not many walks take in the riverbank, for a good deal of its course is without rights-of-way: the river itself leads an uneventful life other than one or two famous moments which all who have visited the dale will already know. Neither are the high tops very inviting, indeed the bulk of Wensleydale's walking is to be had somewhere between the two extremities. The physical structure of the dale gives us a series of regular ledges on which some superb walking can be found. These mid-height terraces also generally provide the best views.

The crowning glory of Wensleydale however (despite the Ure's general lack of interest) are the waterfalls.

5

Nowhere else can boast such a fine array of tumbling waters as this district, for most of the side-valleys also proudly possess their own force and with one notable exception (Cotter Force is not practicably incorporated into any walks, but should be visited separately – find it on the O.S. 2½" map) we visit them all. Yes, these are the gems that make Wensleydale special.

The 16 walks described range from 3½ to 11 miles, and more than half include some upland pasture, if not moorland. All are circular and an average distance of 6½ miles makes them ideal for half-day rambles. Each has its own chapter which includes detailed narrative and strip-map, and notes and illustrations of places of interest.

Although at one end of the dale, Hawes is the major centre, while Aysgarth is probably most central. Market Day at Hawes is Tuesday.

Distances by road from Aysgarth (in miles)

Buckden	9
Grinton	8
Hawes	10
Leyburn	7
Middleham	9
Ripon	27
Sedbergh	25

THE ROAD NETWORK

KEY

• start point
o other village
⌒ 'A' road
⌒ 'B' road
⌒ unclassified road

Scale approx.
5 miles = 1 inch

6

FACILITIES IN THE VILLAGES

	Accommodation	Inn	Car Park	Bus service	Post Office	Shop	Toilets
Appersett			✓				
Askrigg	✓	✓		✓	✓	✓	✓
Aysgarth	✓	✓	✓	✓	✓	✓	✓
Bainbridge	✓	✓		✓	✓		
Burtersett	✓					✓	
Carlton	✓	✓		✓	✓		
Carperby	✓	✓		✓	✓		
Castle Bolton			✓		✓		✓
Countersett	✓						
Coverham			✓				
Gayle	✓			✓		✓	
Hardraw	✓	✓			✓		
Hawes	✓	✓	✓	✓	✓	✓	✓
Horsehouse	✓	✓		✓	✓		
Thornton Rust	✓			✓	✓		
West Burton	✓	✓			✓		
West Witton	✓	✓		✓	✓	✓	
Worton	✓	✓		✓			

Youth hostels can be found at Aysgarth and Hawes. There are also campsites in the Hawes district.
This is a general guide only— if it's important, check it!

ORDNANCE SURVEY MAPS

The strip-maps illustrating each walk will guide one safely around, but show nothing of the surrounding countryside: the obvious answer is an Ordnance Survey map as follows:-

1:50,000 scale
sheet 98: Wensleydale + Wharfedale
sheet 99: Northallerton + Ripon

1 inch to the mile
sheet 90: Wensleydale
sheet 91: Ripon (tiny portion only)

The Outdoor Leisure Map no. 30
'Yorkshire Dales Northern Area'
covers all but two of the walks

PUBLIC TRANSPORT

Wensleydale is not over-accessible by rail. From the east Northallerton is the nearest station, while to the west Garsdale Head on the Settle-Carlisle line can at the time of publication be used. Bus services are a little better, with two United services running up the dale to Hawes. In summer a useful service operates from West Yorkshire via Wharfedale, while very rare services cover Hawes to the Moorcock, and Coverdale, courtesy of Ribble and Handleys of Middleham respectively. It should go without saying that all these details are always liable to change.

INNS AND BEER

Wensleydale has several interesting houses, and most of the sizeable villages have their local. The choice of beers worth drinking is not however too wide. The two brewers common in the area are Theakstons (Masham and Workington) and Youngers (Edinburgh). Fortunately both are usually a safe bet for finding traditional beer. A refreshing change is available in Hawes where three inns stand adjacent, and one purveys the ales of Marstons, of Burton-on-Trent. To keep abreast of changes, one is advised to obtain a copy of 'North Yorkshire Ale', a splendid guide (to much more than the pubs alone) by local branches of the Campaign For Real Ale. For more information ring 0727-67201, the CAMRA headquarters.

SOME USEFUL ADDRESSES

Ramblers' Association
1/5 Wandsworth Road, London SW8 2LJ
Tel. 01-582 6878

Youth Hostels Association
Trevelyan House, St. Albans, Herts. AL1 2DY
Tel. 0727-55215

Yorkshire Dales National Park Office
'Colvend', Hebden Road, Grassington, Skipton,
North Yorkshire BD23 5LB
Tel. Grassington (0756) 752748
Hawes National Park Centre (Old Station Yard)
Tel. Hawes (09667) 450
Aysgarth Falls National Park Centre
Tel. Aysgarth (09663) 424
(both open April to October)

Yorkshire Dales Society
152 Main Street, Addingham,
Ilkley, W. Yorkshire

Yorkshire and Humberside Tourist Board
312 Tadcaster Road, York YO2 2HF
Tel. 0904-707961

United Automobile Company
Grange Road, Darlington, Co. Durham
Tel. 0325-468771

West Yorkshire Road Car Company
PO Box 24, East Parade, Harrogate,
North Yorkshire HG1 5LS
Tel. 0423-66061

The National Trust
36 Queen Anne's Gate, London SW1H 9AS
Tel. 01-222 9251
Membership: PO Box 39, Bromley, Kent BR1 1NH

THE WALKS

Listed below are the 16 walks described, the walk number being the key to easy location in the guide

WALK	TITLE	MILES
1	CASTLE BOLTON AND AYSGARTH FALLS	7
2	THE RIVER BAIN AND THE ROMAN ROAD	$5\frac{3}{4}$
3	HARDRAW FORCE AND PIKE HILL BEACONS	$7\frac{1}{4}$
4	CALDBERGH AND MIDDLEHAM LOW MOOR	$6\frac{1}{2}$
5	AROUND ADDLEBROUGH	$6\frac{1}{2}$
6	IVY SCAR, CARPERBY AND THE URE	$6\frac{1}{4}$
7	THE ASCENT OF WETHER FELL	$5\frac{1}{4}$
8	MOSSDALE AND COTTERDALE	$7\frac{1}{4}$
9	PENHILL BEACON	6
10	HELL GILL AND THE HIGH WAY	$7\frac{1}{4}$
11	AYSGILL FORCE AND GAYLE	$3\frac{1}{2}$
12	NAPPA HALL AND ASKRIGG'S FALLS	7
13	THE WALDEN VALLEY	$6\frac{1}{2}$
14	REDMIRE FORCE AND THE TEMPLARS CHAPEL	$6\frac{3}{4}$
15	SEMERWATER AND RAYDALE	4
16	OVER THE MOORS TO COVERDALE	11

THE WALKS

Outline map showing the routes and the starting points

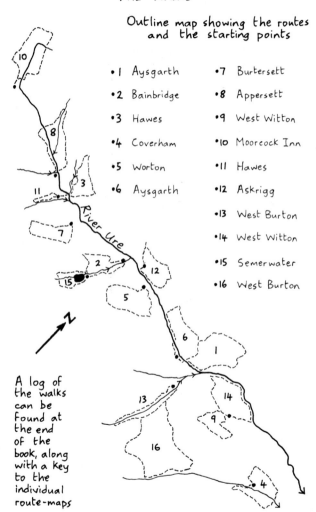

- 1 Aysgarth
- 2 Bainbridge
- 3 Hawes
- 4 Coverham
- 5 Worton
- 6 Aysgarth
- 7 Burtersett
- 8 Appersett
- 9 West Witton
- 10 Moorcock Inn
- 11 Hawes
- 12 Askrigg
- 13 West Burton
- 14 West Witton
- 15 Semerwater
- 16 West Burton

River Ure

A log of the walks can be found at the end of the book, along with a key to the individual route-maps

WALK 1 — CASTLE BOLTON AND AYSGARTH FALLS

7 miles   from Aysgarth

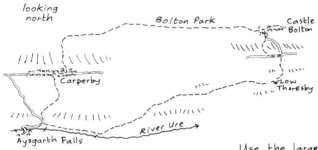

looking north

Bolton Park — Castle Bolton

Carperby

Low Thoresby

Aysgarth Falls

River Ure →

Visits to two of the valley's most famous features, one natural, one the work of man

Use the large National Park car-park at Aysgarth Falls, east of the village.

THE WALK

From the car-park return to the road and turn left under the railway bridge. Within a few yards take a gate on the right, and a path rises through the wood, crossing a wide track to a stile just behind to leave the wood. Head straight up the field, and a string of five gap-stiles guide a sketchy path through the fields, turning left at the last one to emerge onto a farm-lane. Cross straight over and pass through a long narrow field, and after a gate at the end go on a little further to one on the right. Now go left again and a final gate between the houses empties into the centre of Carperby, just opposite the inn.

Turn right for a short distance, taking the first lane on the left. With a 'no through road' sign in evidence it rises out of the village to become a wide enclosed track. Beyond a couple of barns keep right at a fork to accompany the wall round to a gate barring the way. A large tract of rough pasture is entered, and with Bolton Castle in view down-dale our near-level approach to it can be well surveyed.

A generally clear track heads across the pasture to a gate in the opposite wall, then it crosses

12

a beck and heads less clearly along to a gate in the right-hand wall. From here the track becomes wide and clear to lead through half-a-dozen more fields to near the impressive bulk of Bolton Castle. Through a narrow wood the track leads to the very walls of the castle.

Between castle and church we emerge onto a lane alongside the village green, and it is this lane we descend to leave the village. Soon a track forks right between barns. Use it to descend to two houses, behind them crossing the former railway line to eventually join another road. Go left only as far as the Castle Bolton junction, then take a rough track to a barn on the right From the gate by it continue to a stile at the field-end, then bear right down the next field to a stile on the left in the very bottom corner. This leads to a small footbridge onto Thoresby Lane.

Just to the right the lane ends at Low Thoresby, and at a gate just past the farm it becomes a green by-way. This pleasant course is accompanied throughout its entire length: just beyond an extremely wet junction is a gate, and a little further on the track ends with a stile into a field.

Follow the wall away, ignoring the first gate reached and continuing round the wall to a stile by a gate in the far corner. From the gate behind it follow the wall away to another gate, then strike half left over the brow of the field to a stile in the far corner. A farm-track is joined to lead down to Hollin House, keeping right of the first building and going left through a gate before the main grouping. At a gate just beyond the track ends. Head straight across the sloping field to a stile, then a little way along the fence leading away from it drop down left to a stile. Here we join the popular Aysgarth Falls path at its terminus, and just below are the Lower Falls: a gap in the cliffs here permits a descent to the waters-edge. A well-trodden path now heads up-river, passing a short detour to a more intimate viewpoint for the Lower Falls. The path vacates the trees for a while before re-entering to reach the Middle Falls. Only yards further we emerge onto the road just below the car-park.

To include the Upper Falls (best seen from Yore Bridge) turn left along the road to the bridge, from where a footpath leads directly back to the car-park.

Carperby is one of the most attractive and least spoilt villages in the dale. Its depth is virtually non-existant, for all its sturdy stone dwellings line the road running through the village. Standing well back from the valley bottom, it was once of greater importance as testified to by the sizeable market cross. Dating from the seventeenth century it stands at one end of a narrow green. At the opposite end is a good grouping of chapels which have sadly been succumbing to modern trends.

It is claimed that the Wensleydale breed of sheep was first named here.

Carperby market cross

Bolton Castle is a majestic ruin that cannot fail to impress the First-time visitor. When approached from a distance it initially belies its ruinous condition.

Originally a 14th century manor house, it was converted into a castle by Richard, the First Lord Scrope. Mary, Queen of Scots was the most famous guest, being imprisoned here from 1568 to 1569.

The castle is open to visitors and its labyrinthine interior is worth experiencing.

A folk museum and a restaurant add to its attractions. NB: only the village, of course, should have the 'Castle' prefixing the 'Bolton', but the castle often gets the same treatment.

Beldon Beck

②

kiln

...1000

...900

...800

Carperby

inn

①

CASTLE BOLTON

ASKRIGG

Lane

CARPERBY

National Park Centre

Aysgarth Falls

Upper Falls

Middle Falls

former railway station

R. Ure

Lower Falls

Hollin House

⑥

N

...600

...500

inn YH

AYSGARTH VILLAGE A684

WEST WITTON A684

For notes on the Aysgarth area see Walk 6

Although comprehensively overshadowed by its castle, the village of Castle Bolton is highly appealing in its own right. A spacious green separates two intermittent rows of cottages, many of which housed the lead-miners of long ago. Today this is a peaceful place, which like Carperby is well up from the valley bottom. The church of St. Oswalds stands almost at the castle wall. Dating back more than 600 years, this tiny place of worships reveals a surprisingly spacious interior.

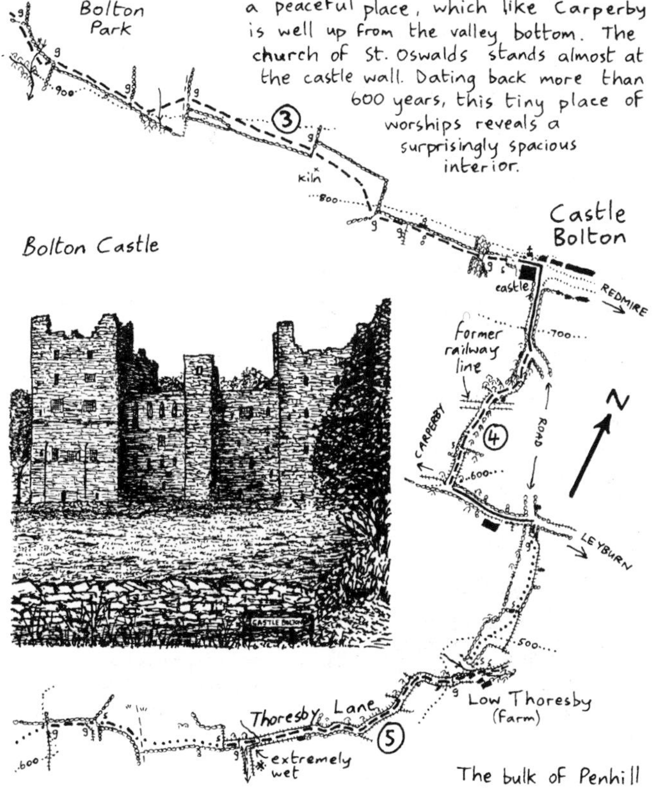

Bolton Park

Bolton Castle

Castle Bolton

former railway line

N

Thoresby Lane

Low Thoresby (Farm)

*extremely wet

Thoresby Lane is a centuries-old byway which feels to have changed little as we follow its enclosed section. At the junction* a fork descends to ford the Ure. Be grateful it's not our route.

The bulk of Penhill is a striking feature of many scenes in the lower dale, and on the descent to Low Thoresby it totally dominates the view directly ahead.

15

WALK 2
5¾ miles

| THE RIVER BAIN AND THE ROMAN ROAD |

from Bainbridge

A steady ramble by the
shortest river and
along an ancient
highway

Park in the
village centre

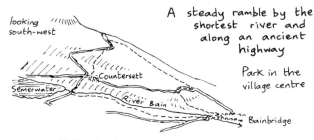

looking
south-west

Countersett
Semerwater
River Bain
Bainbridge

THE WALK

Leave Bainbridge by the main Aysgarth road
at the corner of the green, crossing the bridge over the
River Bain and climbing the steep hill. Leave the road by
a stile on the right just before the junction and head
across the pasture keeping well above the steep drop to
the river. Pass to the left of an 'island' field at the
brow of the hill a sketchy path materialises to lead to
a stile. Marker-posts show the way down the slope beyond,
with Semerwater now fully in view ahead. Continue across
several intervening walls by means of stiles, and on reaching
a ladder-stile bear right to join the nearby riverbank.
Its pleasant course is now followed upstream to shortly
arrive at Semerwater Bridge. Before crossing it, have a
potter along the foreshore of the lake itself: its foot is
directly in front.

To resume the walk, cross the bridge and
climb the steep road to the crossroads at Countersett.
Turn right towards the hamlet, but just before the first
house opt for an enclosed track to some cottages on
the left. Take a gate by the first dwelling on the left
to begin a steep climb to a barn, then up again to
another barn. From it climb half-left to a stile and
continue diagonally to the next top-corner. From the
stile there follow a wall up to a gate to emerge onto
the Countersett–Burtersett road at it's highest point.
Follow it to the right for a couple of minutes to reach
a stile on the right: beyond a collapsed wall head
half-left down the rough pasture to a stile admitting
onto the Roman Road.

Turn right to follow the arrow-like course of the Roman Road to eventually merge into a metalled road. Head up it's gentle slope as far as the farm just ahead, going along it's drive where a stile will be found on the left. Head down the field to a stile at the bottom and across two more fields with a sketchy path linking the stiles. From next to a barn a clearer path leads to the next stile, and our way continues to a stile and then a gate above the river before descending alongside the left-hand wall to a gate. From it a few cottages are passed to re-emerge onto Bainbridge's village green.

Bainbridge is a lovely village whose houses stand well back from an enormous green. Though the main road cuts across it, its effect seems insignificant. The most noticeable features are the stocks which still grace the green, and the whitewashed inn which is always in sight. It dates back several centuries and is possibly the oldest in the dale. The structure which gives the village its name is a shapely platform from which to see not only the best stretch of the river, but the only part before it sneaks quietly round the backs of the houses.

The village has notable historical connections, not least of all with the Romans. Brough Hill, peering over the houses at the east of the village, is the site of the Roman fort Braccium and a handy place to defend, which was no doubt just as well. Some centuries later the Norman lords based their foresters here, when the Forest of Wensleydale was a popular hunting-ground. At the inn can be seen a horn, and during the winter months it was blown at nine o'clock in the evening to guide benighted travellers to safety. Its origin goes back earlier still, as a warning sound in the days of the Forest. Happily this ancient event can still sometimes be seen, surviving purely as a quaint custom. Where our walk re-enters the village is a house that was once the 'Old Dame School', where over a century ago, pupils could learn the 'three R's' for 2d a week (that's 1p to you youngsters!)

Bainbridge : the inn from the green

17

Cam High Road is the Roman Road running from Ribblehead to Bainbridge, and a note about it can be found on page 34. On this walk we tread the easternmost section which points itself unerringly at Bainbridge.

Even in this lower stretch, which is stony underfoot but not rough, the views are very good. An unrivalled length of Wensleydale can be seen, including Hawes, Askrigg, various individual features and most of the surrounding fells. Looking back up the Road, Wether Fell and its outcrop Yorburgh are seen at their shapeliest.

Countersett is a small hamlet with an early Friends Meeting House and a lovely old hall also with strong Quaker connections. The steep slopes above command a superb panorama of Semerwater's side-valley. The best feature is Addlebrough across the valley.

Joining the Ure at Bainbridge, the River Bain is claimed to be the shortest in the country, a point which the Dibb, in Wharfedale would challenge. Our route explores it comprehensively, from the numerous falls over rock ledges above Bainbridge to its so tranquil meander from Semerwater Bridge.

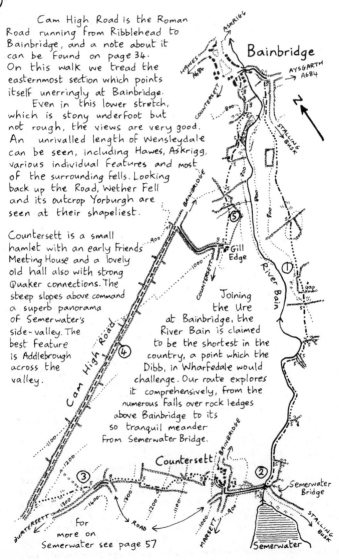

Bainbridge

ASKRIGG

HAWES A684

AYSGARTH → A684

COUNTERSETT

STALLING BUSK

BAINBRIDGE

Gill Edge

COUNTERSETT

River Bain

gap

Cam High Road

Countersett

BAINBRIDGE

Semerwater Bridge

MARSETT

STALLING BUSK

BURTERSETT

ROAD

Semerwater

for more on Semerwater see page 57

18

WALK 3 | HARDRAW FORCE AND PIKE HILL BEACONS |

7¼ miles   from Hawes

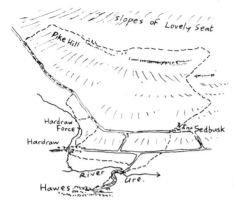

looking
north

A superbly
varied walk
with extensive
views across
Wensleydale

Use the main
National Park
car-park in
the old railway
station yard

THE WALK

From the car-park take the path by the
old railway bridge up onto the road, and turn right to
follow it out of the village. Within a few yards a track
heads off to the left, and with it a gate signals the
route of the Pennine Way, whose flagged course we follow
to rejoin the road a little further on. Continue on the
road as it bridges the Ure, then take a stile which soon
appears on the right. A sketchy path heads across to a
small arched-bridge, then climbs half-right to another stile,
beyond which a large field is crossed to a stile in the
top corner. Cross over the lane to the stile opposite
and resume the rise in the same direction. Two more stiles
quickly ensue before a near-vertical climb to a stile
in the top-right corner. Turn right along the lane
to enter the hamlet of Sedbusk.

Take the lane up between the houses, and
at the top end of the small green bear right as the
lane deteriorates into a rough track. This climbs the
hillside for a good while, and is left by a stile on
the left just before arriving at a gate. A good track
rises up the field, fades a little while passing a tiny
plantation, then reverts to its original form to slope
across to a gate. The track continues to another gate

which gives access to the open fell. Head straight up, keeping left of the small scar, and the path then swings well clear of High Clint (on our left) before curving round onto the plateau above it. The path runs pleasantly along this plateau: at the far end a brief detour is needed to visit the prominent cairn which is a splendid viewpoint with two fine examples of stone men below.

Throughout almost all of this walk we are treading the slopes of Lovely Seat, which rises very gradually above us to 2213 feet.

Rejoin the path and soon after passing a left fork our path peters out. Keep on to another series of cairns, and from them maintain a level course to arrive at Shivery Gill. Cross to a track on the other side and turn left down it to join the unenclosed Buttertubs road. This is accompanied downhill for a good mile and a quarter to the first farm buildings.

Here, at High Shaw, take a lane signposted Fossdale, and within a few yards descend some steps to the heavily-wooded beck. After seeing the waterfall a few yards up, turn left to accompany the beck downstream. Almost immediately a footbridge gives a choice of which bank to follow. Two more small falls are passed before reaching another footbridge. We must leave the beck here to prepare itself for its big moment, which we shall soon be witnessing from below. A path leads up onto the road, but after only a minute to the right it is vacated again at a stile alongside a gate.

A good track heads away and down to West House Farm, and from a stile to its right a path descends two more fields to emerge via a back-yard into Hardraw. If not already aware, the Force is on private land, and access is through the inn where a modest charge is made. Through the inn, a 5-minute walk leads to the impressive amphitheatre of the Scaur. On returning to the inn, cross the road and take a track just left of the bridge. Behind the buildings go left to a small gate from where a good path crosses a number of fields to eventually join a road. Turn right to rejoin the outward route, over Haylands Bridge and back into Hawes.

20

From Sedbusk to Hardraw we enjoy extensive panoramas of Wensleydale. Rising above Hawes are those ubiquitous 2000-footers Wether Fell, Dodd Fell and Widdale Fell. The road to Wharfedale over Fleet Moss (1934') is clearly in sight.

Sedbusk is an unspoilt hamlet of farms and cottages, looking across the dale to Hawes and beyond from an altitude little under 1000 feet. It is so laid back it has even avoided the back-road from Hardraw to Askrigg, being reached only by a narrow lane.

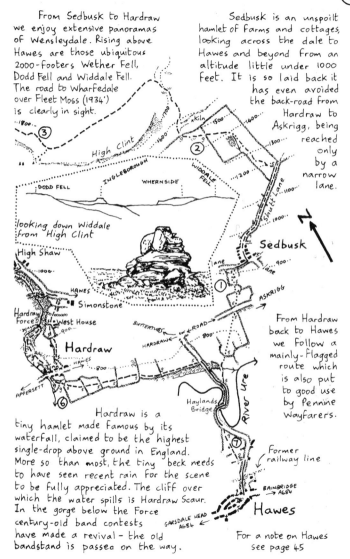

looking down Widdale from High Clint

From Hardraw back to Hawes we follow a mainly-flagged route which is also put to good use by Pennine Wayfarers.

Hardraw is a tiny hamlet made famous by its waterfall, claimed to be the highest single-drop above ground in England. More so than most, the tiny beck needs to have seen recent rain for the scene to be fully appreciated. The cliff over which the water spills is Hardraw Scaur. In the gorge below the Force century-old band contests have made a revival - the old bandstand is passed on the way.

For a note on Hawes see page 45

21

WALK 4

6½ miles

CALDBERGH AND MIDDLEHAM LOW MOOR

From Coverham

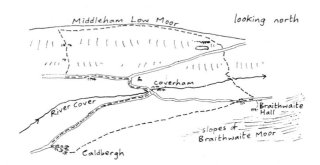

This leisurely ramble takes in several of lower Coverdale's interesting features

Parking can be found at the junction in front of the church, or down the lane just before the bridge

THE WALK

Leave Coverham by crossing the bridge and taking the quiet lane to Caldbergh, turning up into the tiny village on a lane which terminates at the last house. At a gate a farm-track takes over, and is followed along to the left over several cattle-grids to arrive at Ashes Farm. A track then continues across the fields to cease at the second gate reached. From it carry on with a wall on the left: at the next gate the accompanying wall calls it a day. Continue straight across to a gate in a fence, then cross an extensive pasture by passing a plantation before gradually dropping to the very far corner, where a gate empties onto a lane.

Turn right along it, past a farm and on to the drive to Braithwaite Hall with the familiar National Trust sign in evidence. Opposite is a gate from where a track heads away down to the river, interrupted by another gate on the gradual descent. The River Cover is crossed by the stone-arched Hullo Bridge. From it a track heads left up a steep slope, then fades as it rises more gently over a large pasture. At the top a gate precedes the unfenced Coverham-Middleham road over Middleham Low Moor.

Head straight up the slope opposite to join a wide track which can be followed left to a wall-corner. It is worth venturing a little left off this way for a birds-eye view of the whole of Pinker's Pond. At the wall the track begins to fade, and here it can be left by striking a little to the right across the pathless moor. This couldn't be much less like the moors we are used to, and the short-cropped turf is a joy to tread. While keeping an eye open for racehorses the trig. point ahead soon appears, and is attained equally soon.

From it continue along the broad moor-top a good while yet: the boundary wall on the left remains in view for the most part, and on seeing the first set of buildings behind it head in that direction. Do not leave the moor here but follow a track alongside the wall, and within a couple of minutes a solid farm-road is met. This heads through a gate and down to the left, passing between the buildings of Ashgill Stables and alongside those of Tupgill to drop down onto a lane.

Turn left, passing a creamery to return to the junction at Coverham church. The branch right leads straight down to the bridge, but a visit to the attractive church can be included by the lych-gate just in front. A path also leads from its right (south) side down onto the lane to Coverham Abbey, which also merits a look to conclude the journey in style.

Coverham boasts a sylvan setting at the lower end of its dale, and is well and truly off the beaten track Though barely even a hamlet, it has several features of interest. The Abbey was founded by Premonstratensian Canons, and the scant remains include some 14th century arches, now by a private house. Also ancient is the bridge over the Cover, while up above is the church of the Holy Trinity, now no longer in use.

The gatehouse arch, Coverham

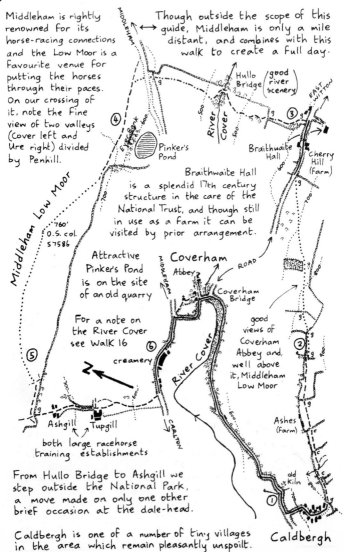

Middleham is rightly renowned for its horse-racing connections and the Low Moor is a favourite venue for putting the horses through their paces. On our crossing of it, note the fine view of two valleys (Cover left and Ure right) divided by Penhill.

Though outside the scope of this guide, Middleham is only a mile distant, and combines with this walk to create a full day.

MIDDLEHAM

Hullo Bridge (good river scenery)

EAST WITTON

River Cover

Braithwaite Hall

Cherry Hill (Farm)

Braithwaite Hall is a splendid 17th century structure in the care of the National Trust, and though still in use as a farm it can be visited by prior arrangement.

Middleham Low Moor

760' O.S. col. 57586

Pinker's Pond

Attractive Pinker's Pond is on the site of an old quarry

For a note on the River Cover see Walk 16

Coverham Abbey

MIDDLEHAM

Coverham Bridge

ROAD

good views of Coverham Abbey and, well above it, Middleham Low Moor

creamery

River Cover

CARLTON

Ashgill Tupgill

both large racehorse training establishments

Ashes (Farm)

old kiln

From Hullo Bridge to Ashgill we step outside the National Park, a move made on only one other brief occasion at the dale-head.

Caldbergh is one of a number of tiny villages in the area which remain pleasantly unspoilt.

Caldbergh

WALK 5

6½ miles

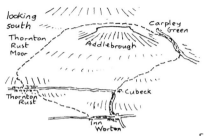

looking south
Thornton Rust Moor
Thornton Rust
Addlebrough
Carpley Green
Cubeck
Inn Worton

AROUND ADDLEBROUGH

from Worton

A straightforward circuit of this shapely fell, with outstanding views of the district

Park in the spacious lay-by opposite the inn, on the Aysgarth road out of the village.

THE WALK

Head back into the village and turn left at the first junction up the steep lane to Cubeck. Turn right into the farming hamlet and then immediately left up a steep track enclosed by walls. At a gate the track runs more freely, sloping across a field and then steeply up to a gate at the top corner. Beyond it the track fades away: head across to a gate over to the right, after which the path sketchily re-appears to continue it's now-level course. The path heads across to a gate, then accompanies a wall away to emerge onto the cul-de-sac lane to Carpley Green: turn left.

Just prior to reaching the first barn, take a gate on the left to follow a wall away to another gate. A large pasture is entered and with no visible path simply contour across it, keeping roughly parallel with the wall down to the right. On rounding to a gate a sketchy path materialises to reach another gate and continues on to a gate in the right-hand wall. The path now surmounts a vague ridge to head towards a stile. Across it, the expanse of Thornton Rust Moor is entered and our reasonable path strikes out half-left across the undulating terrain. On reaching a gate the track descends to enter walled confines which channel our steps unerringly down into Thornton Rust village.

Turn left along the lane as far as the edge of the village, then take a small gate on the right labelled Nipe End. From a stile just below, a path leads through the trees to emerge via a stile into a field. Here the

Final leg begins, a pathless trek through pleasant fields taking in no less than a dozen gap-stiles in rapid succession. The only potentially confusing one is the first, found in the crumbling wall half-left of our emergence from the trees. This is the general direction taken to eventually reach the main road: the inn at Worton is now only minutes along to the left.

Addlebrough is a classic table-topped fell that seems to crop up in almost every Wensleydale view. Modest crags line its northern side, and help to accentuate the abrupt edge of the plateau. The Brigantes are thought to have occupied a hill-fort here - no doubt in stark contrast to the Roman fort in the valley bottom.

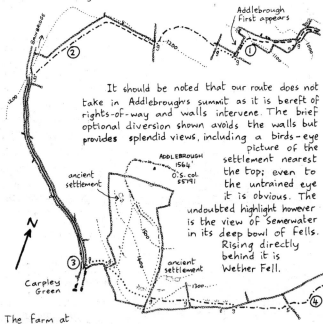

It should be noted that our route does not take in Addlebrough's summit as it is bereft of rights-of-way and walls intervene. The brief optional diversion shown avoids the walls but provides splendid views, including a birds-eye picture of the settlement nearest the top; even to the untrained eye it is obvious. The undoubted highlight however is the view of Semerwater in its deep bowl of fells. Rising directly behind it is Wether Fell.

The farm at Carpley Green stands at the end of the road as far as motor traffic is concerned, but an old packhorse way continues over the Stake to the Kidstones Pass and Wharfedale, a splendid route for walkers.

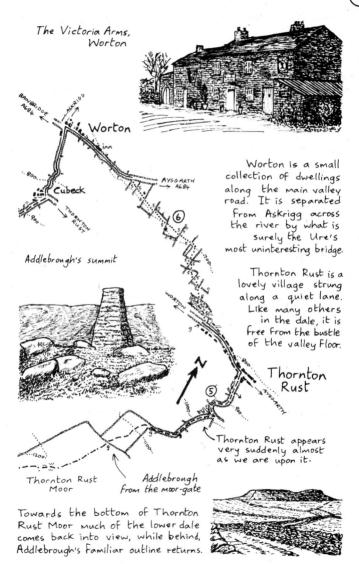

The Victoria Arms,
Worton

Worton is a small
collection of dwellings
along the main valley
road. It is separated
from Askrigg across
the river by what is
surely the Ure's
most uninteresting bridge.

Thornton Rust is a
lovely village strung
along a quiet lane.
Like many others
in the dale, it is
free from the bustle
of the valley floor.

Thornton
Rust

Addlebrough's summit

Thornton Rust appears
very suddenly almost
as we are upon it.

Thornton Rust   Addlebrough
Moor   from the moor-gate

Towards the bottom of Thornton
Rust Moor much of the lower dale
comes back into view, while behind,
Addlebrough's familiar outline returns.

27

WALK 6

$6\frac{1}{4}$ miles

IVY SCAR, CARPERBY AND THE URE

from Aysgarth

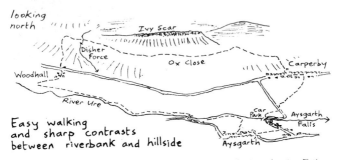

looking north

Ivy Scar

Disher Force

Ox Close

Carperby

Woodhall

River Ure

Car Park

Aysgarth Falls

Aysgarth

Easy walking and sharp contrasts between riverbank and hillside

Use the information-centre car-park over the bridge at the Falls

THE WALK

Leave the car-park at the opposite end to the entrance to find a footpath leading down to the bridge by the upper falls. Cross it and climb the steep road as far as a stile on the right. An intermittent path goes across the fields, keeping generally level and squeezing through a multitude of identical gap-stiles. On the edge of Aysgarth village the path drops to a gate to join a back lane which is accompanied up to the Methodist church on the edge of the green.

This is also the point where the village is left, through a narrow gap between houses on the right. A path descends through two stiles and down alongside a wall, using a stile in it to cross half-right to another stile to reach an old mill. Stiles on it's left lead onto an enclosed track which is followed left until it swings up the hill: here leave it by a stile on the right. Beyond a barn a stile gives access to a pleasant path through trees by the river, emerging to continue to a stile where river and road converge. Continue along the road for a very short distance to arrive at a long, narrow footbridge which we use to cross the Ure.

A stile on the left marks the commencement of a long, easy stretch along the riverbank. This pathless trek clings to the river to become confined in a rough section between wall and river. On emerging we this time stay with the wall, crossing a small beck as the wall parts company before reaching a stile. Continue on the same line to the next stile to join a farm-track. Head right, under a former railway bridge, up through the hamlet of Woodhall and out onto the Carperby – Askrigg road.

Cross straight over and pass between house and barns opposite to use a farm-track to climb the steep field. Towards the top of the steep section take the lesser track branching right to the gate just ahead. The day's climbing is now done, and a good, level track runs along to the right, through a gate to the ford at the top of Disher Force. A brief detour (no right-of-way) through the gate just before the ford provides an excellent view of this fine waterfall.

From the gate behind the ford, our track heads across Ox Close Pasture to the old lead mines under the shadow of Ivy Scar. Weaving through the spoil heaps the track emerges at the far end to continue on it's way a little sketchily. On eventual arrival at a gate, swing right to drop to a gate in the far corner, descending similarly on a farm-track through another field. After passing the remains of old quarries the track falls to a gate on the right, and continues straight down through two fields. Half-way down the second of these look for a stile on the left, and from it cross a field-bottom to another stile. Descend this narrow pasture, through two gates by farm buildings and out onto the lane in Carperby.

Turn left along the main street as far as the handily-sited inn, and then opt for a gate opposite it to enter a narrow field between houses. Leave it by the first gateway on the right, continuing down this field to a stile at the very bottom. It admits onto a farm-lane which is crossed straight to another stile. Follow a wall away to another stile from where an intermittent path heads half-right across several fields, with a string of traditional gap-stiles serving to indicate the course.

Soon a wood is entered: cross straight over the main track through it, and a path leads half-right down onto a road. Turn left, underneath the former railway bridge and the Falls car-park is immediately on the right.

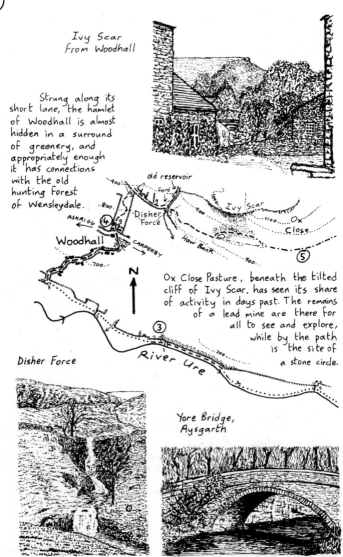

Ivy Scar
from Woodhall

Strung along its
short lane, the hamlet
of Woodhall is almost
hidden in a surround
of greenery, and
appropriately enough
it has connections
with the old
hunting forest
of Wensleydale.

old reservoir

ford

Ivy Scar

Disher
Force

Ox
Close

ASKRIGG

Woodhall

CARPERBY

Haw Bank

N

Ox Close Pasture, beneath the tilted
cliff of Ivy Scar, has seen its share
of activity in days past. The remains
of a lead mine are there for
all to see and explore,
while by the path
is the site of
a stone circle.

River Ure

Disher Force

Yore Bridge,
Aysgarth

The village of Aysgarth stands high above the river, and has a spacious air about it. A small green flanks the main road which divides the village. Aysgarth however stands quite aloof from the attraction that brings visitors in their tens of thousands to this corner of the dale, its famous waterfalls. Half a mile east of the village is the series of Upper, Middle and Lower Falls which make Aysgarth famous. Here the Yoredale series of rocks make their greatest showing to create a water-wonderland. It is the grand scale of things rather than their height that provides the spectacle. What makes all this truly *beautiful* is the setting — thickly-wooded with rich plant-life. The best viewpoint for the Upper Falls is Yore Bridge, a gracefully tall single-span structure. Originally from the 16th century, it has since been much-widened.

Yore of course is the older name for the river Ure.

For a note on Carperby see page 14

The large building adjacent to Yore Bridge is a former spinning mill, now being used to house the Yorkshire Carriage Museum. Up the steep hill behind is the Parish Church of St. Andrew. Restored last century, only the tower base of this very large church remains from medieval times. Inside are two fine 15th and 16th century screens.

To help complete the scene at Aysgarth Falls, one can also find an inn, a youth hostel, a gift-shop, a cafe and a National Park Centre at the car-park on the north bank.

31

WALK 7

THE ASCENT OF WETHER FELL

5¼ miles

from Burtersett

looking south

Cam High Road

Wether Fell

Yorburgh

Burtersett

A well-defined climb combined with a bracing stroll along a Roman road

There is reasonable parking alongside the lane just above the sharp bend at the village head

THE WALK

From the sharp bend at the top end of the village (by the tiny green), take the 'no through road' branching to the right at the very corner, alongside a chapel. Almost at once it forks, and our track climbs to the left leaving the last cottage behind and heading up a steep slope. This wide track is still used by the farmer and is therefore easy to follow, climbing the hillside and always sloping to the right. On gaining equal height with the prominent upthrust of Yorburgh just to the left, ignore a fork right to a gate and continue straight up: shortly the nearby wall at last leaves us for good, and the track, briefly a little less clear, crosses level ground to a gateway.

Beyond it the track improves again and a sunken green way climbs across the fellside. Ignoring lesser branches left and then right, the track arrives at the last gate of the climb. Ahead is the summit of Wether Fell, but the inviting track heading towards it should be treated with contempt: within five minutes it will lead the unfortunate walker into dark, deep peat groughs, definitely not recommended. Instead then, accompany the wall along to the right, passing the old quarry on Flint Hill and being greeted by new views across to the west. This rather more circuitous course should not be hastily abandoned: our sketchy path heads ever nearer the top and the temptation to strike out to the left is best avoided until the slope there becomes invitingly steep. At the same time as this our wall-side way becomes much wetter, path-less and generally less appealing. Climbing the grass to the left some peat groughs are encountered at the top, and now the summit cairn appears only a couple of minutes beyond. A level grassy stroll completes a relatively dry ascent.

To begin the return journey head down the only significant drop from the summit to join the wide track of the Roman Road just to the south. This well-trodden route is now followed for quite a distance on it's gentle descent towards Bainbridge, soon becoming fully enclosed at a gate. The location of our departure from it is about a mile beyond the gate, where a footpath sign at a stile indicates the way to Burtersett. A sketchy path slopes down to a stile from where the sketchy path is left in favour of an invisible one straight ahead. A stile is reached just left of a wall-corner. A few yards further and Burtersett appears: the way is now obvious, passing through a broken wall down to the bottom corner of a plantation and through three more stiles to emerge onto the lane where we began.

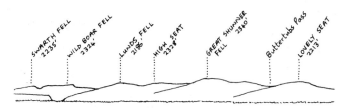

SWARTH FELL 2235' WILD BOAR FELL 2324' LUNDS FELL 2186' HIGH SEAT 2328' GREAT SHUNNER FELL 2340' Buttertubs Pass LOVELY SEAT 2213'

looking north-west from the summit

Wether Fell is a rare venture for us, a climb to 2000 feet. This 'rush of blood' is due to the ease by which this fell can be conquered: Wensleydale's other mountains are set much further back from the valley and constitute a far greater challenge.

The summit is known as Drumaldrace, and is probably as good a viewpoint for the Dales mountains as anywhere.

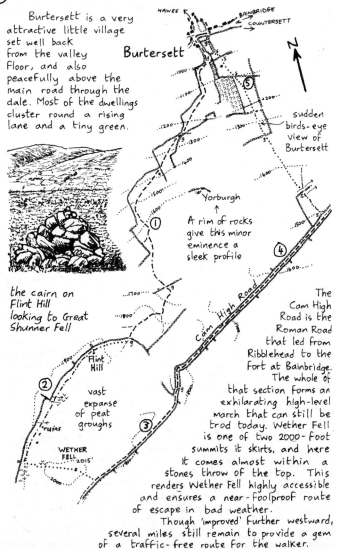

Burtersett is a very attractive little village set well back from the valley floor, and also peacefully above the main road through the dale. Most of the dwellings cluster round a rising lane and a tiny green.

Burtersett

sudden birds-eye view of Burtersett

↑ Yorburgh
A rim of rocks give this minor eminence a sleek profile

the cairn on Flint Hill looking to Great Shunner Fell

vast expanse of peat groughs

ruins

Flint Hill

WETHER FELL 2015'

Cam High Road

The Cam High Road is the Roman Road that led from Ribblehead to the fort at Bainbridge. The whole of that section forms an exhilarating high-level march that can still be trod today. Wether Fell is one of two 2000-foot summits it skirts, and here it comes almost within a stones throw of the top. This renders Wether Fell highly accessible and ensures a near-foolproof route of escape in bad weather.

Though 'improved' further westward, several miles still remain to provide a gem of a traffic-free route for the walker.

WALK 8

7¼ miles

from Appersett

Gentle walking
through two
secluded valleys

Park alongside the
green, near the bridge

THE WALK

From the green cross the adjacent road-bridge
over Widdale Beck and just beyond a barn take a stile
on the left. Walk parallel with the road as far as the
next bridge (this time over the Ure) but stay in the field
and cross a stile to follow the Ure up-dale. On emerging
from trees forsake the riverbank and slope up the field:
pass along the top of the trees, over a stile and across
a large hollow to eventually reach a stile into the woods.
Descend to cross a tiny beck as it enters the river, then
head left to a barn. From the gate there carry on to a
farm track, which bends left to a gate by another barn.

This track is followed only to the next gate,
where instead of continuing up to Birk Rigg Farm, fork left
on another track through the gate in front. The track is
now followed through four further gates. When it swings to
the left to climb through low outcrops to Mid Mossdale Farm,
leave it and head on to the far end of the field. Now
simply follow the river upstream, past a farm-bridge to a
wedge of trees deflecting us from the water. At a gate in
the next substantial wall a sketchy farm-track strikes left
to the now-prominent Mossdale Head Farm.

Pass to the right of the main building to use
the bridge over Mossdale Beck. From it ignore the various
tracks left and right, and instead climb the field with a
wall on the right. Through a gateway head right to a gate
in the fence on the right: follow the fence striking right,
and when it swings away continue on to a steep slope

35

down to the A685 at Thwaite Bridge. Cross straight over road and bridge and up a path through the trees. From a stile at the top climb diagonally up the steep pasture to a stile at the top-right corner, then continue across a gentler slope to locate a stile in a long wall climbing the fell. From it make similarly for the next one, from where a steady descent can be made to the unfenced road in Cotterdale. Turn left along this quiet lane into the hamlet of Cotterdale.

On nearing the last buildings leave the road by a footbridge, crossing two fields to obvious gap-stiles. Then accompany a tiny watercourse to the next stile and continue along a field-bottom. At a collapsed intervening wall strike left up a pronounced grassy rake to a stile in the top wall.

continued across

Cotterdale

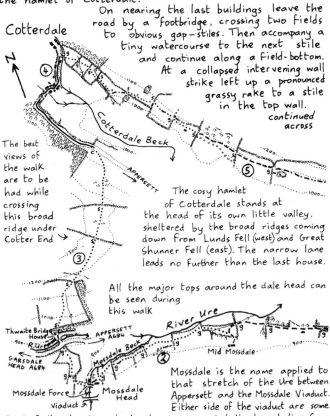

The best views of the walk are to be had while crossing this broad ridge under Cotter End

The cosy hamlet of Cotterdale stands at the head of its own little valley, sheltered by the broad ridges coming down from Lunds Fell (west) and Great Shunner Fell (east). The narrow lane leads no further than the last house.

All the major tops around the dale head can be seen during this walk

Mossdale is the name applied to that stretch of the Ure between Appersett and the Mossdale Viaduct. Either side of the viaduct are some lovely falls. The 4-arch structure once carried the branch line from Hawes to Garsdale Head (then Hawes Junction) on the Settle-Carlisle line.

Turn to follow the wall to a stile by a barn and a gateway below the next barn. Our way now continues on a level course through some varied pastures. Having given us a brief clear spell the path becomes indistinct beyond the crumbling walls of an extensive fold: at the very end of the pasture rise to a gap-stile, then keep right of a short length of wall on a sheep-trod contouring round towards a stile. From it contour yet again to join a wide track descending to a gate. From the stile by it head down the now-enclosed track only as far as the first gate on the right.

Descend by a wall to a stile, then head down across a large field to the wall at the very far end. Find a gate a few yards up to the left then drop down to a more conspicuous gate in the next wall. Aim now for a stile in front of roadsigns which indicate arrival at the Hardraw junction of the A685.

Turn left along the main road, almost immediately crossing Ure Bridge and soon re-entering Appersett via the bridge over Widdale Beck.

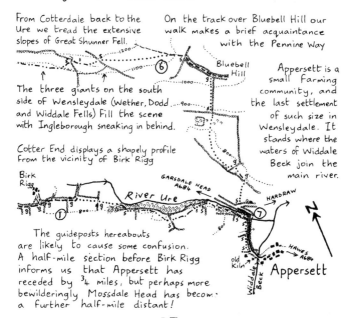

From Cotterdale back to the Ure we tread the extensive slopes of Great Shunner Fell.

On the track over Bluebell Hill our walk makes a brief acquaintance with the Pennine Way

The three giants on the south side of Wensleydale (Wether, Dodd and Widdale Fells) fill the scene with Ingleborough sneaking in behind.

Appersett is a small farming community, and the last settlement of such size in Wensleydale. It stands where the waters of Widdale Beck join the main river.

Cotter End displays a shapely profile from the vicinity of Birk Rigg

The guideposts hereabouts are likely to cause some confusion. A half-mile section before Birk Rigg informs us that Appersett has receded by ¾ miles, but perhaps more bewilderingly Mossdale Head has become a further half-mile distant!

WALK 9

6 miles

PENHILL BEACON

From West Witton

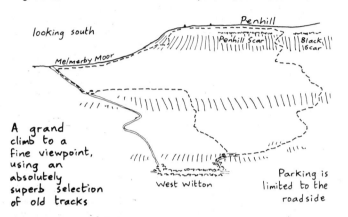

looking south

Penhill

Penhill Scar

Black Scar

Melmerby Moor

A grand
climb to a
fine viewpoint,
using an
absolutely
superb selection
of old tracks

West Witton

Parking is
limited to the
roadside

THE WALK

Leave West Witton by a lane at the west (Aysgarth) end of the village, by a small grass triangle opposite the former school. Leaving the last dwellings behind it climbs to a crossroads of tracks: go straight ahead and the lane becomes an enclosed track to rise past an old quarry before arriving at a junction with a splendid green road (High Lane). Take the gate in front and resume the rise on a sketchy green track, passing through two more gates before emerging onto the broad plateau directly under the cliffs of Penhill.

Our green path heads left before we fork away from the wall to cross to the most distant of the four spoil-heaps. From there double back along the tops of the three other prominent spoils, exploring as you go. At the last one a path (only one of many hereabouts) rises just behind it, and gently climbs an expertly-engineered sunken way to the edge of Penhill's summit plateau.

Turn left alongside the wall to a stile, and continue on a sketchy path along the edge, passing the trig. point over the wall before arriving at a small cairn. Only a little further on is the big cairn overlooking the eastern slopes. From it our descent over Melmerby

Moor is well laid-out, as is the alternative bridleway through the fields to the left. A path drops immediately away from the beacon to a stile in the wall-corner below, but the steepness can easily be by-passed by the various paths in the vicinity. From the stile a good path stays fairly close to the wall to cross the moor to join the Melmerby-West Witton road at its highest point.

Go left over the cattle-grid and down to Penhill Farm, after which leave the road by a track along to the left known as Flint Lane. Its level course is trod as far as a stile a short distance beyond a prominent clump of trees, from where a steep field is descended to a stile onto a similar green lane. From the stile opposite drop through two more fields onto a third and final green lane.

Turn left to a barn then bear right across the field behind to a stile. Be sure to peer over the fence ahead to see the waterfall in the wood, then take a wicket-gate to the left. A path crosses the caravan-site to leave by a similar gate, then descends steeply through the trees onto the very lane by which we departed the village. Turn right, therefore, to re-enter West Witton.

Penhill is Wensleydale's best-known fell, its ability to stand out in views from afar outpointing its popularity as a climb. When its top is gained, it is usually by a quick stroll from a car at the top of Melmerby Moor. Its abrupt northern/north-eastern edge however renders Penhill as easily identifiable from most parts of Wensleydale, and it is a regular feature of views westward from the North York Moors.

Penhill's own virtues as a viewpoint are assisted by the dramatic plunge of the Scar, the top of which provides near-birds-eye pictures of the lower dale. It is the aforementioned advantages which have given the hill historical significance. It was the site of a beacon, one of a chain throughout the land which when lit could rapidly spread the message of some impending danger. The coming of the Spanish Armada was of course top of the list. Something which is less certain is that this was also the location of an Iron Age chieftain's last resting-place.

Strictly speaking, the true summit of Penhill is a mile to the south-west of the Ordnance column, but an hour-long return plod is not recommended. To clarify what exactly is what on the summit plateau, the true top is over 1800', the O.S. column is at 1727', and the small cairn on the mound (the beacon site) is 1685'. To the east, and a little lower still is the big cairn on Penhill End.

West Witton is a pleasant village sadly split almost in two by the incessant traffic racing through. On the slopes of Penhill, it looks out across the valley from high above the river. The village is perhaps best known for an annual event here, the burning of Owd Bartle. An effigy, presumably of Saint Bartholomew to whom the church is dedicated, is joyfully burnt in Guy Fawkes fashion.

The meaning of this seems to have gone up in the smoke of the years

West Witton

LEYBURN A684

AYSGARTH A684

waterfall

caravan site

Green Gate

Penhill Farm

AGGLETHORPE

N ←

MELMERBY

④

Melmerby Moor

⑤

Flint Lane

A study of the map reveals a range of alternative routes - both the green roads of High Lane and Flint Lane allow the walk to be cut, while a choice also exists along the top.

For a look at the summit see page 39

Penhill End   cairn
③
beacon

Penhill Scar

PENHILL 1727'
O.S. column
57708

← old quarry (now an eyesore of a tip)

①

High Lane

The section from under Penhill Scar onto Melmerby Moor is not an official right-of-way, but stiles are provided at the only two obstacles, and as long as we behave we should have no problem.

②

x spoil heap   Black Scar

Evidence of local industry in the form of lead mining and quarrying are much to be found hereabouts

WALK 10

7¼ miles

HELL GILL AND THE HIGH WAY

from the Moorcock Inn

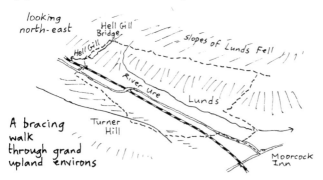

looking
north-east

Hell Gill
Bridge

Hell Gill

Slopes of Lunds Fell

River Ure

Lunds

Turner
Hill

Moorcock
Inn

A bracing
walk
through grand
upland environs

There is ample parking in the vicinity of the inn at the junction
of the Kirkby Stephen road with the Hawes — Sedbergh road

THE WALK

From the inn head down the Kirkby Stephen road
and leave it by a farm-track on the right towards Yore
House. After crossing the Ure (choice of two bridges) turn
left on a sketchy track upstream. This soon fades, but
continue to a farm-bridge from where a track leads to
Blades Farm. Pass between the buildings and at the end
take a gate to the right. A track crosses the field to
another gate, and a detour through two more leads to
the steep pasture behind. When the track fades climb
straight up to a gate, and maintain this course through
three more fields up to the derelict farm of High Dyke.
Use gates to its right to get onto the open fell.

Running alongside the intake-wall is a track: this
is the High Way and it leads us on a generally-level
course all the way to Hell Gill Bridge. For the most part
the wall stays with us. When it eventually parts company
the track continues on to the top of a line of trees
above a gorge. Sketchily the way continues by small
outcrops to join a wide green track just before getting
to Hell Gill Bridge.

On crossing the bridge take the track on the
left to descend past farm buildings and down through
the fields. A little before crossing the railway bridge onto

the road, be sure to deviate right a few yards for a splendid view of Hell Gill Force. On joining the road at Aisgill Moor Cottages cross straight over to a gate and from it follow the fence left to a wall. Though pathless the way is straightforward, remaining fairly level with a wall as company again for the most part. Beyond the barns at High Shaw Paddock the last gate is encountered before entering a large tract of rough pasture.

While crossing this pasture gain height gently to arrive at a small beck, ideally just at the top of its steepest section. Further across is a wall which is followed uphill to gain the south ridge of Swarth Fell at a gate. Turn left with the wall over the gentle rise of Turner Hill and then down as far as a gate in the wall.

From the gate descend a rather rough pasture to a highly prominent footbridge over the railway line. A track heads away from it to rejoin the road, and the Moorcock Inn is only a few minutes along to the right.

Turner Hill is an excellent viewpoint, chiefly for the fine surround of fells. Besides a good length of railway, the best single feature is the entire length of Wensleydale stretching away.

Blades is the only farm we encounter which is still operating. The prominent white building on the hillside above-left is the former youth hostel.

High Dyke was once an inn catering for travellers on the old road.

The Moorcock's strategic position places it in that small band of well-known (from the outside at least) outpost-hostelries.

Turner Hill
1521'

Moorcock Inn

Blades

High Dyke

old Kiln

SEDBERGH A684
HAWES A684
SETTLE
CARLISLE
KIRKBY STEPHEN B6259
River Ure

This walk is a real treat for railway enthusiasts, the famous line being visible much of the time. Just south of the cottages is Aisgill Summit, at 1169 feet the highest point on a main line in Britain.

Aisgill Moor Cottages

KIRKBY STEPHEN 80659 CARLISLE

④

Hell Gill Force

This splendid waterfall makes a vertical drop over a cliff, and youngsters should be kept on a tight rein.

GARSDALE HEAD 80259 SETTLE

→ Z

1300 1200

High Shaw Paddock

Hell Gill Bridge is a sizeable stone-built structure over an unexpected gem. The beck, source of the Eden, rushes through a deep, dark and narrow ravine. The old Yorkshire–Westmorland border (and modern equivalent) follows the beck down to the road. From the bridge to the cottages we make our only foray out of the county, into what is now Cumbria. In this area the National Park also shares the boundary

Hell Gill Beck

1200

Hell Gill

Hell Gill Bridge

1300

③

This last beck before Hell Gill Bridge is in fact the infant Ure, here within 1½ miles of its birthplace on Lunds Fell. The rugged little gorge is one of its few lively moments outside of Aysgarth.

High Hall

1300

1300 The old High Way

High Way

The old Kiln

②

1300

The High Way is part of the route taken by Lady Anne Clifford on the way to her Westmorland castles. Now a route for more leisurely travellers, it once formed the major 'highway' through the valley

Wild Boar Fell (2324') from Aisgill Moor

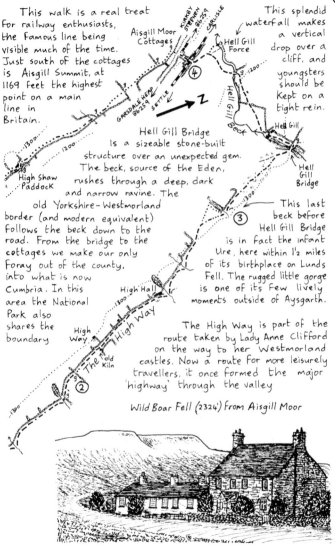

WALK 11

3½ miles

| AYSGILL FORCE AND GAYLE |

from Hawes

looking south-west

A simple stroll in the valley of Gayle Beck

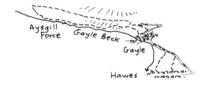

Aysgill Force   Gayle Beck

Gayle

Hawes

Use the main National Park car-park in the old station yard

THE WALK

Leave Hawes through the small car-park on the main street almost opposite the Board Inn. From a stile in its left corner a sketchy path rises half-right across two fields to join the Gayle road adjacent to the large creamery. Turn left up into the heart of Gayle, and after leaning on the bridge to survey the falls on Gayle Beck take the short cobbled way to the right, continuing along a lane to an old kissing-gate after the last house on the left. Climb half-right past a wall corner and on to a stile with Pennine Way signs in residence. Continue at the same angle as before to a stile above the beck, then descend to its bank.

The way is now straightforward, with Gayle Beck being followed upstream to Aysgill Force. Beyond the waterfall remain with the beck past two footbridges, the second by a barn. At the end of the next field we leave the beck by rising right to join a farm-track at a gate. This green track is followed to the right, soon becoming enclosed and eventually becoming a lane after a gate by a barn on a bend. A few yards further is a stile from where the Pennine Way is traced back to Hawes.

Firstly two fields are crossed, and from the stile we used earlier turn left to accompany a wall down onto a lane. Almost immediately then use the lane joining it to drop down onto the edge of Gayle. The Way then avoids the village centre by branching left across two fields, passing between modern housing to emerge onto the lane to Hawes. Turn briefly left

Hawes is the 'capital' of upper Wensleydale, the lively colourful market town to which all visitors are drawn. The place gains even more character on its market-day when there are, happily, as many local people to be seen as tourists. Once the last stop on the Wensleydale branch line, the station has now been put to good use as a National Park Centre. Alongside it in the old station yard is the Upper Dales Folk Museum, where one can learn of the old local industries, including probably the best-known, that of cheese-making. Hawes has retained an unconventional layout, including some cobbled road, and a leisurely exploration really is needed. Other buildings include the parish church of St. Margaret, and a modern youth hostel at this major staging-post on the Pennine Way.

THE WALK continued and then leave by a barn on the right. A flagged footpath leads through two fields to arrive at the parish church. Take the path to its left, through its yard and out onto Hawes main street.

Note the profusion of field-barns above Gayle

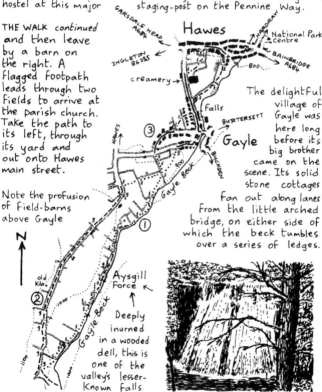

The delightful village of Gayle was here long before its big brother came on the scene. Its solid stone cottages fan out along lanes from the little arched bridge, on either side of which the beck tumbles over a series of ledges.

Hawes

National Park Centre

GARSDALE HEAD A684
INGLETON B6255
MUKER A684
BAINBRIDGE A684

creamery

falls

BURTERSETT

③

Gayle

HAWES

BUCKDEN

800

700

Gayle Beck

①

N

old kiln

②

1000

1100

1000

Gayle Beck

Aysgill Force

Deeply inurned in a wooded dell, this is one of the valley's lesser-known falls

WALK 12 | NAPPA HALL AND ASKRIGG'S FALLS |

7 miles   from Askrigg

Park in the centre of Askrigg

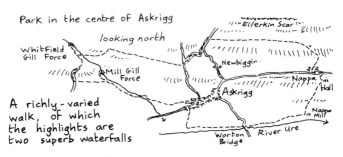

A richly-varied
walk, of which
the highlights are
two superb waterfalls

THE WALK

From the village centre follow the Hawes
road out of the bottom end of the village, and after
the last house on the left take a track down past
an animal feeds works. From the gate at the bottom
pass between the ramparts of a former railway bridge
and continue in the same direction through a series
of five stiles. From the last a sketchy path heads
straight for the river, but instead of following it to
the bank turn left on a low embankment to arrive
at a stile in a wall-corner. Follow the fence away
from it (parallel with the river) to a gate from where
the riverbank is at last joined. Accompany the Ure
downstream to soon emerge onto a road adjacent to
the characterless Worton Bridge.

At a stile opposite continue down the
river. A footbridge, gate and second footbridge lead
to a gate behind which is Nappa Mill Farm: take
the farm-drive up to the left, but leave it by a
stile on the right just before crossing the beck.
Climb diagonally away to the right-hand gate of
two, and continue in the same direction to another
gate admitting to the environs of Nappa Hall. Take
the enclosed track up past the Hall and out onto
the road.

Turn left along the road only as far
as the first branch right (signposted 'no through road)
and head through the hamlet of Nappa Scar. Stay
on this lane which at the top of the hill becomes

an unmade track: it now swings left for a long and pleasant level march to debouch onto a lane rising out of Askrigg. Turn down towards the valley, ignoring a lane left, a track right and another lane right (to Muker). Just below is another walled track, and this we follow along to the right. Remain on it throughout its entire length, and just before it escapes into a field take a stile on the left. Whitfield Gill Force immediately appears through the trees directly below. Our route must take a circuitous course in order to stand at its foot, for the steep slopes prevent a direct descent. Instead, the path heads downstream high above the wooded beck before dropping down to a footbridge, then rises to meet the path to the waterfall. Turn upstream to arrive at the fall, care being needed as this can be a slippery path.

To resume the walk retrace steps to the path junction and then continue straight on to a stile. This recently created route has replaced a path which previously had to deviate from the beck, but now we can accompany the numerous yellow blobs downstream. A side beck and then a stile are encountered before the way skirts above the walled, wooded beckside, only to then enter the trees at a stile which soon appears. Very quickly we are to be deposited back into a field to continue down, meeting another stile before one returns us to the trees.

The path runs along the top of the trees to a junction, and here the second detour to our second waterfall is made, the wooded confines being almost a replica of the situation already experienced further up the beck. This time however it is but a very brief stroll along a much better path upstream to witness the delights of the equally impressive waterfall of Mill Gill Force.

After admiring the cascades return to the path junction and continue downstream on an excellent path along the top side of the wood, with the bonus of a distant view across the main valley in addition to peering into the gill itself. At the bottom end of the wood two neighbouring stiles lead to a footbridge across the beck, and within a few yards our track forsakes the beck to pass to the left of an old mill, under a modest aqueduct to a stile. A flagged path then leads to a lane which in turn takes us back into the centre of Askrigg.

Askrigg is a wonderfully different village, seeming of another age to the 'typical' Dales village. Formerly a market town and a famous clockmaking centre, Askrigg gradually gave way to Hawes as centre for the upper dale.

The village centre still clearly recalls those days: the market cross, the three-storeyed houses along the main street and the 15th century St. Oswald's church with its splendid old beams. Flat-topped Addlebrough is prominent in the Askrigg scene.

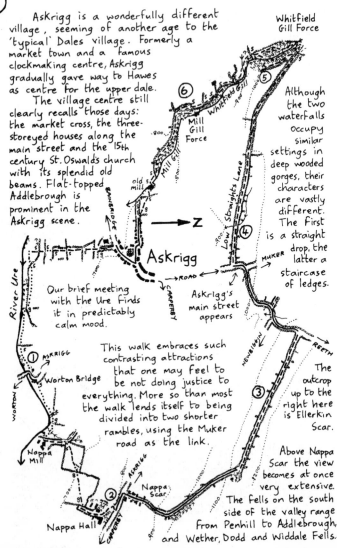

Whitfield Gill Force

Although the two waterfalls occupy similar settings in deep wooded gorges, their characters are vastly different. The first is a straight drop, the latter a staircase of ledges.

Our brief meeting with the Ure finds it in predictably calm mood.

Askrigg's main street appears

This walk embraces such contrasting attractions that one may feel to be not doing justice to everything. More so than most the walk lends itself to being divided into two shorter rambles, using the Muker road as the link.

The outcrop up to the right here is Ellerkin Scar.

Above Nappa Scar the view becomes at once very extensive. The fells on the south side of the valley range from Penhill to Addlebrough, and Wether, Dodd and Widdale Fells.

Whitfield Gill Force

Mill Gill Force

Nappa Hall dates from the mid-fifteenth century, and was a fortified manor house of the influential Metcalfe family. It is now a farm, and a peep through the entrance arch reveals the scene below. Note the stunning carpet of snowdrops in the adjacent wood (in the season!)

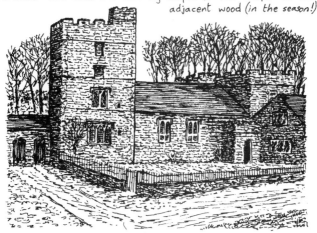

WALK 13

6½ miles

An intimate exploration
of an unfrequented
side-valley. Almost
gradient-free

looking
south-east

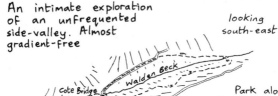

Park alongside
the village green
but *not* on the grass

THE WALK

     Leave the village-green by a narrow lane
signposted to 'Walden only'. When it forks take the left
arm towards Walden South, and after passing a barn
take a stile on the right. Here a long pathless trek
begins across the sloping fields above Walden Beck. Follow
the wall away from the road to a stile in it, then
commence a level walk which calls for little description:
every intervening wall is graced with a stile
     The first deviation from this occurs after
a good mile, when a wall deflects us half-right across
a field with a beck in it. From the stile there the rise
continues over a fenced pasture, beyond which a small
gate precedes a footbridge over Cowstone Gill. Pass to
the right of the house, over a stile and head across
the field to a gate opposite. Through it join a farm-
track to enter the confines of Hargill Farm. From the
right-hand building cross the tiny beck to a footgate,
and then resume the level hike across the fields.
This is maintained through several more stiles before
descending to the next farm, Bridge End. At this most
distant point of the journey, take a stile to the right
of the buildings to round them to a small farm-bridge
over Walden Beck.
     On the opposite bank take a stile found
immediately on the left, and continue downstream to a
stile in a fence. Now the beck is left by climbing half-
right to a gate at the top-corner. From it turn left to

commence a long, level march to complement that on the outward leg. Again virtually pathless, the way this time is broken up mostly by gates, and before long the farm of Whiterow appears ahead. Pass along the front of the buildings and the access-road takes over to guide us out onto a lane. Turn left to accompany this ultra-quiet lane for a long mile until arriving at Cote Bridge over Walden Beck.

　　Without crossing it take the gate on the right, and follow the beck down as far as a footbridge across it. Once again forego the crossing, and this time head half-right away from it to a stile. Rise up the side of the next field to a stile half-way, then break across a field to an easily-located gapstile. Now head straight across three more fields in a direct line: beyond that a track descends left, but we branch off it to a stile just before it reaches a gate. Follow the left-hand wall around to a final stile and descend the edge of a field to a small gate on the left. Steps lead down to a footbridge below West Burton Falls, which can be enjoyed at a closer range before turning right to re-appear back on the village green.

　　The Walden valley is one of the least-known and least-changed in the Dales, and the reason certainly for the former, is that it is a dead-end for motor vehicles. Not only that, the quiet lanes that set off up each side of the valley fail to connect again, thereby denying any circular tour. The individual farms are the only settlements up-dale of West Burton. The beck flows a good 7 miles to reach the village, being born under the summit of Buckden Pike.

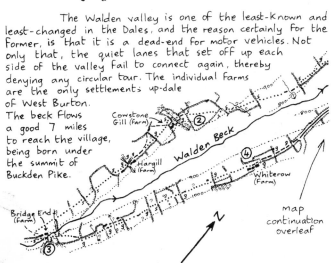

map
continuation
overleaf

West Burton is an absolute gem of a village, not only well away from the main road through Wensleydale but also hidden from the lesser road that runs through Bishopdale to join it. Strictly speaking the village is in the Walden valley, and jealously guards the only entrance to it. Outstanding is the extensive green, with cottages stood back in appreciation. An obelisk of 1820 stands on market-cross steps, with village stocks nearby: 'round the back' are the delightful falls in a wooded dell. This is surely Wensleydale's best!

West Burton

BUCKDEN B6160 ← → AYSGARTH

inn

West Burton Falls →

600

⑥

WALDEN HEAD

Riddings

⑦

① Cote Bridge

Cote (Farm)

Walden Beck

⑤

Whiterow Road

600 700 800 900

Where a track joins the lane just before Cote Farm note the remains of a chimney and flue of a smelting mill of a former lead-mine.

West Burton Falls

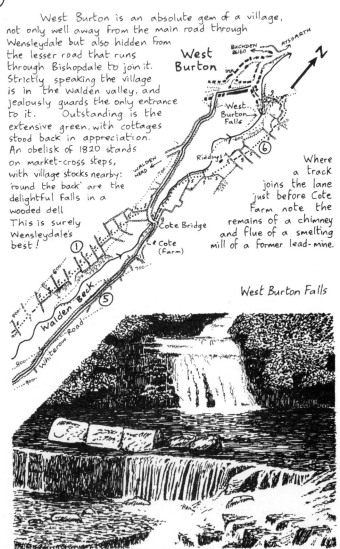

WALK 14 | REDMIRE FORCE AND THE TEMPLARS CHAPEL |

$6\frac{3}{4}$ miles   from West Witton

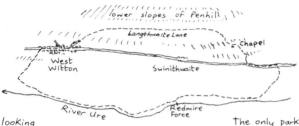

looking
south

**Easy walking and easy
route-finding. Included
is the best long section
of riverbank in the valley**

The only parking is
along the main street, with
the best place being found
at the eastern end of the
village. Here there is a wide
verge just after the last
houses on the left. This is
also where the walk begins.

THE WALK

From the east (Leyburn) end of the village
take a walled track just after the last house on the
left. Almost at once it forks: take the right-hand option.
Twisting and turning, this way leads steadily downhill
towards the river, becoming narrower in it's latter stages.
At the very end do not take the obvious gate directly
in front, but opt for the one just to the right. In the
field cling to the left-hand boundary wall, until it's many
indentations lead down to a gate with the river now in
close proximity. Cross the stream behind the gate and
drop to another gate in the fence to the right.
        The riverbank is now joined, and plain-
sailing ensues as the Ure is followed up-dale through
a succession of gates in pleasant pastures. Eventually,
beyond a large wooded island and a lively bend, a
wall commences to separate us from the river. Stay with
the wall, crossing an intervening stile and continuing
on to a stile hidden in the very corner of the next
field. From it a good path heads through the trees,
and almost immediately the grandeur of Redmire Force
greets the eye.
        Almost as soon as it reaches the Falls,

53

the path climbs a stairway away from the river to a stile out of the woods. A field is crossed to another stile and then the right-hand wall leads through several more fields. High above the river the route follows a fence to two neighbouring stiles from where the fence heads across an extensive pasture. When it bends away continue straight ahead to a stile in the far corner.

A good path drops through the trees to briefly rejoin the river, but on emerging into a large riverside pasture we finally leave the river with the wall curving up to the left. A partially-enclosed track materialises to lead up onto the main road. Turn left along it almost to the first farm, then take a stile on the right to follow a farm-track to the top end of the field. From a gate it climbs through trees, and a stile on the left at the top gives access to the remains of the Knights Templars Chapel.

From here follow a now sketchy track to a gate at the top of the field, going on to join a concrete farm-road.

continued across

Redmire Force

River Ure

③

.500

inscribed stone near the chapel *

T 1865

N

.500

④

Temple

WEST WITTON A684

Temple Farm

Templars Chapel

.600

AYSGARTH A684

.700

AYSGARTH / BOLTON

boundary post (Aysgarth/Leyburn) and also an inscribed stone similar to the one depicted, to be seen by the gate above the chapel.

.800

⑤

Langthwaite Lane

The Chapel of the Knights Templar is a little less exciting than it looks on the map. Here the low ruins of the chapel of the Penhill Preceptory include several graves, the structure itself dating from the early thirteenth century. Several adjoining buildings remained uncovered when this was excavated in 1840.

here Penhill appears directly above, looking moody and menacing in the right conditions.

The roadside Temple (all very confusing this) was built in 1792 as a belvedere by the owners of nearby Swinithwaite Hall.

Follow the farm-road uphill only as far as a pronounced bend right, then head up a vague track to the top of the field. From a gate in an angle of the wall head across the now-level pasture to another gate. Now with a wall on the right, accompany it as far as a stile which gives access to the terminus of a green lane.

This is Langthwaite Lane, and all is plain sailing as this superb way is trod all the way back to West Witton. Towards the end it becomes a little rougher and finally joins a narrow tarmac lane to descend into the village.

Despite being a major valley of the Dales, Wensleydale only attracts large numbers to its river at a very short stretch at Aysgarth. This much less-known section however provides outstanding company for several beautifully-wooded miles.

On descending Back Lane note the stately Bolton Hall on the opposite bank. Set in graceful parkland, this home of the Lords Bolton dates back three centuries.

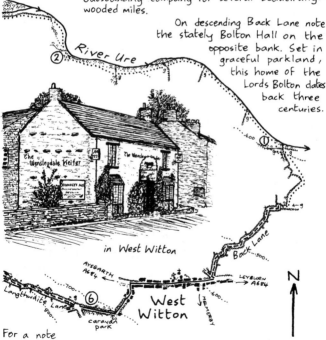

in West Witton

For a note on West Witton see page 40

WALK 15

SEMERWATER AND RAYDALE

4 miles   from Semerwater

A very easy circuit
of Semerwater.

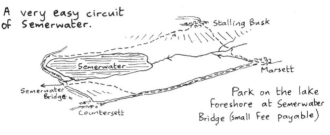

Park on the lake
foreshore at Semerwater
Bridge (small fee payable)

THE WALK

From the foreshore of the lake head along
the lane away from the bridge (not over it) and at
the foot of a hill take a stile on the right, just
opposite a farm. Maintain a level course across the
fields, taking in several stiles to emerge very close
to the lake-shore. By now a good path has materialised
and it heads gradually upwards across rough pastures
alongside the head of Semerwater. More stiles ensue
to arrive at the ruined chapel of Stalling Busk. A
stile is provided to enable a look-round. Only yards
beyond it the barely-evident path forks: head up to
the left on an improving path alongside a small beck.
It leads unerringly up onto the cul-de-sac road in
the hamlet of Stalling Busk.

Walk only a few yards to the right, and
before a sharp bend take a rough track down to the
right. This enclosed way takes us down to a ford over
Cragdale Water, then heads away, forsaking it at a
bend (by a footbridge) to cross two lesser becks directly
ahead. Beyond, the track becomes enclosed to enter
Marsett alongside Marsett Beck. Cross the green to
the road-bridge, and follow this quiet, level lane for
about one and a third miles. Shortly after a brief climb,
journeys end beckons at the lake-foot, and as the lane
descends a stile on the right admits to a field. Follow
the tiny beck down to a gate: once through it the
beck is crossed, and a short muddy section through the
trees leads to a gate adjacent to Semerwater Bridge
which is crossed to complete the walk.

Semerwater was the largest lake in the old North Riding of Yorkshire, and in a district not over-endowed with sheets of water it has become a popular venue for a variety of water-sports. An Association exists to control the activities and help protect bird-life. Near the lakeFoot is the Carlow Stone, once dropped by a giant.

The best-known legend of the district relates how a visitor, inhospitably treated, caused a whole 'city' to disappear under the waters. What seems a little more certain is that Iron Age lake-dwellings existed here.

The old church at Stalling Busk stands in strange isolation some 200 feet below the hamlet. The ruins romantically overlook the lake, and exude an atmosphere not felt at the replacement St. Matthews up by the houses.

If one's boots should still be clean on leaving Marsett, a potentially squelchy finish can be avoided by remaining on the lane to the Countersett road-junction, and there turning right.

Both Marsett and Stalling Busk are peaceful farming hamlets, Marsett in the valley bottom and Stalling Busk perched on the hillside with good views of the lake.

Marsett

Stalling Busk

A cul-de-sac for motorists, but the start of a good walkers' track over to Wharfedale.

The side-valley containing Semerwater has no satisfactory name, though Semerdale has sometimes been offered as a makeshift title. Above the lake it is generally referred to as Raydale, this being the central, the largest and the only level one of the three valleys which merge between Marsett and Stalling Busk. Bardale and Cragdale are the lesser two.

WALK 16   OVER THE MOORS TO COVERDALE

11 miles   from West Burton

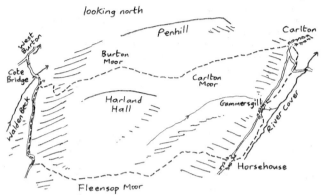

looking north

West Burton · Penhill · Carlton · Burton Moor · Cote Bridge · Carlton Moor · Harland Hall · Gammersgill · River Cover · Walden Beck · Horsehouse · Fleensop Moor

An invigorating if mildly strenuous walk, using two fine inter-valley paths on high moorland to visit two Coverdale villages. Not surprisingly the views are extensive.

Take your sandwiches and make a day of this one!

There is reasonable parking just beyond Cote Bridge, which is reached from West Burton by the lane to 'Walden only'. Fork left at the first junction and the lane descends to the bridge. If walking from West Burton, use the map in Walk 13 to reach and return from Cote Bridge. This adds an extra 1½ miles.

THE WALK

Leave Cote Bridge by the lane heading up the valley, and remain on it's traffic-free course for about 1¼ miles. Above a steep rise a guide-post indicates the departure of a bridle-road to Horsehouse. Take this track to the left, passing through a gate and rising across the slope to swing left to a gate onto the moor-top. Now virtually level a good path heads away, but after a short distance be sure to opt for the less-clear left path at a fork. It crosses the undulating moor to a gate, there becoming clear again to reach the headwaters of the Fleensop valley.

At another junction fork right to a gate, and after fording Fleemis Gill the track rises past grouse butts to a gate on the left. The last section of moor is crossed more sketchily to arrive at and follow a wall along to the left. Use the first gate in it to begin the drop into Coverdale. Head down the pasture finally veering left to a stile in the bottom corner, then make use of the walled confines of a wooded beck to descend into Horsehouse.

Turn right only as far as the inn then take the lane running behind it for a few yards, to leave it by a gate down to the right. Descend to another gate, left to yet another and then cross to a small gate right of a barn. The River Cover is joined and accompanied downstream for some distance. Several intervening fences are crossed and beyond a wooded bend the path squeezes between fence and river, but the gates at either end of the field by-passed provide an easier passage.

In the next pasture we leave the river behind by taking a gate at the far end and heading up the field to the next gate. Continue up to a stile well to the right of the farm buildings, and a wooded enclosure leads onto the road through Gammersgill. Turn right as far as the second field after the beck, then take a gate on the right and bear left to a stile. A green lane is entered and this delightful narrow byway is followed to its terminus.

On emerging into a field continue across to a wall-corner then across again to the top far end of the next pasture. A beck is crossed to a well-hidden stile

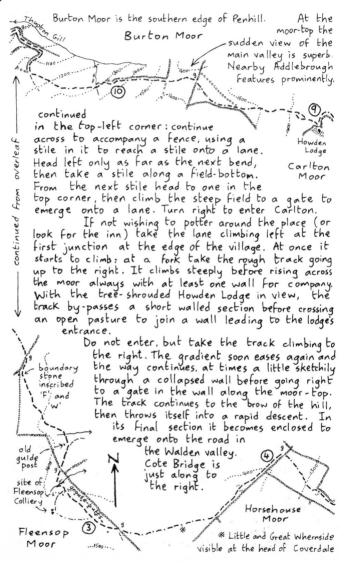

Burton Moor is the southern edge of Penhill.   At the moor-top the sudden view of the main valley is superb. Nearby Addlebrough features prominently.

Burton Moor

Thupton Gill

Howden Lodge

Carlton Moor

continued in the top-left corner: continue across to accompany a fence, using a stile in it to reach a stile onto a lane. Head left only as far as the next bend, then take a stile along a field-bottom. From the next stile head to one in the top corner, then climb the steep field to a gate to emerge onto a lane. Turn right to enter Carlton.

If not wishing to potter around the place (or look for the inn) take the lane climbing left at the first junction at the edge of the village. At once it starts to climb: at a fork take the rough track going up to the right. It climbs steeply before rising across the moor always with at least one wall for company. With the tree-shrouded Howden Lodge in view, the track by-passes a short walled section before crossing an open pasture to join a wall leading to the lodge's entrance.

Do not enter, but take the track climbing to the right. The gradient soon eases again and the way continues, at times a little sketchily through a collapsed wall before going right to a gate in the wall along the moor-top. The track continues to the brow of the hill, then throws itself into a rapid descent. In its final section it becomes enclosed to emerge onto the road in the Walden valley. Cote Bridge is just along to the right.

boundary stone inscribed 'F' and 'W'

old guide post

site of Fleensop Colliery

N

Fleensop Moor

Horsehouse Moor

* Little and Great Whernside visible at the head of Coverdale

continued from overleaf

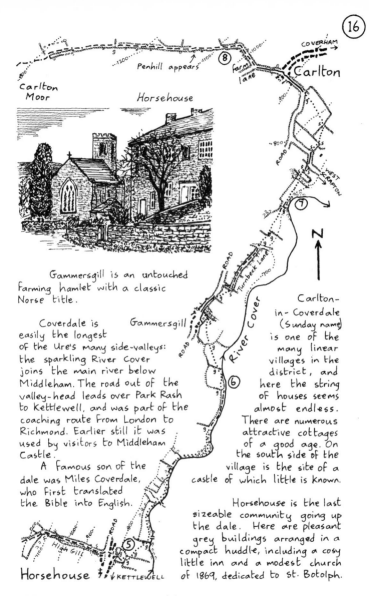

COVERHAM →

Penhill appears ↑

⑧ farm lane

Carlton

Carlton Moor

Horsehouse

WEST SCRAFTON →

⑦

N ↑

Gammersgill is an untouched farming hamlet with a classic Norse title.

Coverdale is easily the longest of the Ure's many side-valleys: the sparkling River Cover joins the main river below Middleham. The road out of the valley-head leads over Park Rash to Kettlewell, and was part of the coaching route from London to Richmond. Earlier still it was used by visitors to Middleham Castle.

A famous son of the dale was Miles Coverdale, who first translated the Bible into English.

Gammersgill

ROAD

Turnbeck Lane

River Cover

⑥

ROAD

Carlton-in-Coverdale (Sunday name) is one of the many linear villages in the district, and here the string of houses seems almost endless. There are numerous attractive cottages of a good age. On the south side of the village is the site of a castle of which little is known.

Horsehouse is the last sizeable community going up the dale. Here are pleasant grey buildings arranged in a compact huddle, including a cosy little inn and a modest church of 1869, dedicated to St. Botolph.

High Gill

ROAD

⑤

Horsehouse ↓ KETTLEWELL

LOG OF THE WALKS

These two pages provide an opportunity to maintain
a permanent record of the walks completed

WALK	DATE	TIME Start	TIME Finish	WEATHER	COMMENTS	
1						
2						
3						
4						
5						
6						
7						
8						

WALK	DATE	TIME Start	TIME Finish	WEATHER	COMMENTS
9					
10					
11					
12					
13					
14					
15					
16					

KEY TO THE MAP SYMBOLS

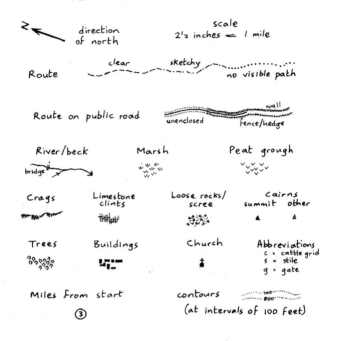

scale
2½ inches = 1 mile

direction of north

Route — clear — sketchy — no visible path

Route on public road — wall — unenclosed — fence/hedge

River/beck — bridge

Marsh

Peat grough

Crags

Limestone clints

Loose rocks/scree

Cairns summit other

Trees

Buildings

Church

Abbreviations
c = cattle grid
s = stile
g = gate

Miles from start
③

contours
(at intervals of 100 feet)
700
800

THE COUNTRY CODE

Respect the life and work of the countryside
Protect wildlife, plants and trees
Keep to public paths across farmland
Safeguard water supplies
Go carefully on country roads
Keep dogs under control
Guard against all risks of fire
Fasten all gates
Leave no litter - take it with you
Make no unnecessary noise
Leave livestock, crops and machinery alone
Use gates and stiles to cross fences, hedges
and walls